JUL   2013

Kids Making a Difference

Helping Others

Elizabeth Raum

Chicago, Illinois

www.capstonepub.com
Visit our website to find out more information about Heinemann-Raintree books.

To order:
☎ Phone 800-747-4992
🖥 Visit www.capstonepub.com
to browse our catalog and order online.

Edited by Nancy Dickmann and Laura Knowles
Designed by Victoria Allen
Picture research by Mica Brancic
Illustrations by HL Studios

Originated by Capstone Global Library, Ltd
Printed and bound in China by CTPS

16 15 14 13 12
10 9 8 7 6 5 4 3 2 1

Library of Congress Cataloging-in-Publication Data
Raum, Elizabeth.
Helping others / Elizabeth Raum.
    p. cm.—(Kids making a difference)
Includes bibliographical references and index.
 ISBN 978-1-4329-6501-3 (hb)—ISBN 978-1-4329-6506-8 (pb)
1. Young volunteers in social service—Case studies—Juvenile literature. 2. Young volunteers in community development—Case studies—Juvenile literature. 3. Voluntarism—Juvenile literature. 4. Social service—Juvenile literature. 5. Humanitarianism—Juvenile literature. I. Title.
HQ784.V64.R38 2013
361.0083—dc23   2011039440

Acknowledgments
The author and publisher are grateful to the following for permission to reproduce copyright material: Alamy pp. 5 (© Jim West), 13 (© kpzfoto), 24 (© Leonid Plotkin), 21 (© Claude Thibault); Ashlee Smith pp. 29, 30, 31; British Red Cross p. 12 (UNP/Peter Sandground); Cans for Kids p. 7; Corbis pp. 4 (ZUMA Press/© Ton Koene), 6 (epa/© Craig Lassig), 15 (Reuters/ © Adrees Latif), 27 (Sygma/© John Van Hasselt), 33 (ZUMA/The Commercial Appeal/© Mike Maple), 38 (© Peter DiCampo/VII Mentor Program), 41 (Demotix/Demotix/ © Mahmoud illean); Glosmedia.co.uk p. 10 (Robert Davis); iStockphoto p. 37 (© Sean Warren); Katie Stagliano pp. 17, 18, 19; newhallschool.co.uk p. 9; Ryan's Well Foundation pp. 35 (www.ryanswell.ca), 36 (www.ryanswell.ca); Sandra Dyas p. 40; UNICEF p. 23 (India/Graham Crouch); © UNICEF/NYHQ2008-1517/ p. 26 (Milaine Ibanga).

Cover photograph of volunteers building a house reproduced with permission of Corbis/© Tim Pannell.

Background design images supplied by Shutterstock/Toria/ZeroTO/silver-john.

Every effort has been made to contact copyright holders of material reproduced in this book. Any omissions will be rectified in subsequent printings if notice is given to the publisher.

Disclaimer
All the Internet addresses (URLs) given in this book were valid at the time of going to press. However, due to the dynamic nature of the Internet, some addresses may have changed, or sites may have changed or ceased to exist since publication. While the author and publisher regret any inconvenience this may cause readers, no responsibility for any such changes can be accepted by either the author or the publisher.

Contents

In their own words

Look for these boxes to find inspirational quotes from the kids featured in this book and other famous people who made a difference.

Kids who made a difference

These boxes tell you stories about kids who have done great things to make the world a better place, both now and in the past.

Top tips

Search for these boxes for quick facts about how you can make a difference.

Some words in the book are in bold, **like this**. You can find out what they mean by looking in the glossary.

So Many Ways to Help

Helping others is fun. It is rewarding, too. Young people help others every day, often beginning by helping at home. Perhaps you help by doing the laundry, preparing meals, or taking care of younger brothers and sisters.

Many young people reach out to their neighbors. Simple acts of kindness make a big difference. Older people may need help running errands or caring for their yards. They may be lonely. Just waving and saying "hello" can make a difference.

Keeping your neighborhood safe is important, too. Something as simple as reporting broken glass in a play area may prevent other children from getting hurt. Being a good example to younger children is also helpful.

In Kenya, these Maasai girls help to do the family laundry.

These children are working with a charity to prepare meals for needy families in Michigan.

Kids who made a difference

Jimmy Carter began helping out on his father's farm when he was only five or six years old by carrying drinking water to the farmworkers. When he was older, he helped care for the animals and protect the cotton crop from insects. Helping others became Jimmy Carter's lifelong goal. He served as president of the United States from 1977 to 1981. Later, he set up the Carter Center, an organization that helps fight disease and hunger in Africa and Asia.

In their own words

Aesop, a storyteller in ancient Greece, wrote a fable called "The Lion and the Mouse." The **moral** of the story is, "No act of kindness, no matter how small, is ever wasted."

Helping the community

Young people can help others by working with organizations such as the American Cancer Society, children's hospitals, or the Red Cross. Groups such as the Boy Scouts, Girl Scouts, and other clubs often take part in **community service projects**.

Sometimes young people pitch in to help their communities at times of crisis. During floods, such as the 2011 flood in Fargo, North Dakota, schoolchildren played a major role in helping to build **dikes** to hold back floodwaters. Younger children helped fill sandbags and passed out water and food to workers. Everyone pulled together to save the community. After a disaster, such as a flood, hurricane, or tornado, young people may also help with the cleanup.

These young people are helping to make sandbags for dikes to save Fargo, North Dakota, from flooding in 2011.

These teenagers are recycling aluminum cans.

Recycling

In Cyprus, an island in the Mediterranean Sea, teenagers help others through a project called Cans for Kids. They sort out aluminum cans at a **recycling** center. Companies buy the recycled aluminum, and Cans for Kids uses the money to purchase medical equipment for a children's hospital. The teenagers are helping the environment as well as sick children.

Top tips

Some projects, such as recycling, need everyone's help. Recycling and picking up litter help the entire community. Find out about recycling projects in your community. If there is an aluminum can or plastic bottle recycling project that pays for recycled items, you can donate the money you earn to your favorite cause.

School projects

Many schools hold **fund-raising** events to help others. In the United States, many schools participate in "Trick-or-Treat for **UNICEF**," **sponsored** by the **charity** UNICEF (the United Nations Children's Fund). Students who go trick-or-treating on Halloween carry an orange UNICEF box door-to-door, asking for **donations**. The money helps UNICEF provide medicine, food, safe water, education, emergency relief, and more to children in over 150 countries.

There are dozens of ways to help. Some take only a few minutes, while others require hours of effort. Students around the world entertain people in hospitals or nursing homes. They help younger children with schoolwork or do errands or gardening work for elderly neighbors.

In their own words

Doctor and thinker William James (1842–1910) had an outlook on life that we can still learn from today. He said, "Act as if what you do makes a difference. It does."

Helping Haiti

Many schools have raised money to help the victims of the 2010 earthquake in Haiti. At one New York City high school, students paid a fee to play basketball against their teachers. They sent the money to help rebuild Haiti.

This schoolgirl is taking part in a lunch club for the elderly.

Tackling big problems

While many children help in their homes, schools, and neighborhoods, some young people have taken helping others a step further. They have learned new skills such as **first aid** or gardening in order to help their neighbors. Others are making a difference by tackling serious problems like hunger, child labor, or water shortages in faraway places. Read on to meet some of these amazing kids.

Top tips

Check to see if your school supports a particular charity. If so, get involved. If not, get together with friends and suggest a project to your principal. Make sure to do your research first. It is best to have a workable plan before you begin.

Matt Pearce: Saving Lives

Matt Pearce, age 15, was delivering newspapers when he noticed that one of his regular customers had left her door wide open. Matt looked inside to see if everything was all right. He found Joan Robson, an 84-year-old woman, clinging to the doorframe. Her speech was slurred.

"I was studying first aid in school and I recognized her **symptoms**," Matt said. "I thought it was a stroke right away." A stroke occurs when the blood flow to the brain is interrupted or reduced. Symptoms include trouble walking and talking, headaches, blurred vision, or numbness on one side of the body or face. Strokes may cause brain damage or even death. Prompt medical treatment reduces the risk of death and brain damage.

Matt Pearce's quick action saved an elderly neighbor.

Matt helped Mrs. Robson to a seat and promised not to leave her alone. Then he called an ambulance. When it arrived, he helped the **paramedics** care for Mrs. Robson. Matt later visited her in the hospital. She recovered completely, thanks to Matt's quick response.

Matt lives in Longlevens, Gloucester, in southern England, as shown on this map.

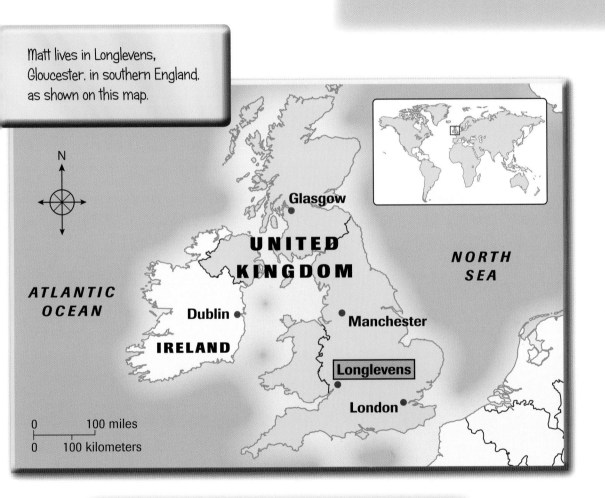

Helping again

A few days later, Matt and a friend were walking along a nearby street. Matt noticed a man sitting on the ground. Later, Matt described the situation: "His speech started to slur, too, and I thought he was having a stroke . . . so I called the ambulance again." Thanks to Matt's quick response, the man received the medical care he needed.

Heart attack

Dionne Burns took a Red Cross first aid class in her hometown of Glasgow, Scotland. After she completed the class, she volunteered to help out at a 2.5-mile (4-kilometer) race. One of the runners, Ian Kennedy, suffered a heart attack at the finish line, and he stopped breathing. Dionne knew exactly what to do. She called for help, and then she used a special lifesaving machine to shock his heart. He started breathing again and, within a short time, paramedics arrived and took over. Dionne's training and her quick action saved Ian's life.

Seventeen-year-old Dionne Burns saved the life of Ian Kennedy, who collapsed after a cross-country race.

First aid classes teach life-saving skills.

The Red Cross and local hospitals offer a variety of first aid classes for young people and adults. Some classes teach workplace and school safety. Others teach people how to respond to common accidents, as well as to life-threatening emergencies such as strokes or heart attacks. The Red Cross also offers babysitting classes to prepare young people to care for younger children.

Top tips

Take a first aid or water safety class. You'll not only help yourself, but you may have the opportunity to help someone else, too.

Screaming for help

It is important to be aware of what is going on around you. Matt Pearce noticed something was wrong, so he called for help. Jared Vigil, of Louisville, Colorado, didn't see a problem; he heard one. On February 6, 2008, 14-year-old Jared heard screaming on his way home from school. He wasn't sure if it was an animal or a person, so he stopped and looked around. That is when he realized that his neighbor, Connie Ostwald, had fallen into an icy pond. Jared called 911, then he adjusted the straps on his backpack and used it to pull the woman out of the freezing water.

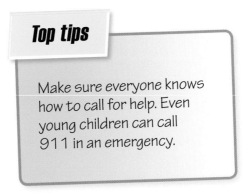

Top tips

Make sure everyone knows how to call for help. Even young children can call 911 in an emergency.

Staying safe

Matt, Dionne, and Jared did everything right. As soon as they realized that someone was in trouble, they called for help. It is important to let others know there is a problem as quickly as possible. Paramedics, firefighters, and police have the training and equipment to help in emergencies.

These kids also knew that the first rule in rescue is personal safety. An injured rescuer cannot help anyone else. That is why Jared stayed safely on dry land. Wading into the icy water would have been dangerous.

Tilly Smith, shown here reading a poem, has been called the angel of the beach because her tsunami warning saved so many lives.

Kids who made a difference

British schoolgirl Tilly Smith, age 10, traveled to Thailand with her family in December 2004. Tilly, who had just studied **tsunamis** in school, noticed the early warning signs on the beach. She warned everyone to run for safety. Her warning saved more than 100 tourists from the killer wave.

Katie Stagliano: Feeding the Hungry

Katie Stagliano's dream of helping others began with a cabbage seed. Every child in her class received one seed, thanks to a program in her school that gives cabbage plants to children in third grade. Katie planted her seed in her yard. She watered it and fed it plant food to make it grow well. Katie's grandfather helped her build a sturdy wire cage around the cabbage plant to protect it from deer. The cabbage grew . . . and grew . . . and grew. It eventually weighed in at 40 pounds (18 kilograms)!

Katie lives in Summerville, South Carolina, as shown on this map.

A growing idea

Katie wanted to do something special with her cabbage. Her mother contacted Fields to Families, an organization that helps farmers get crops to groups that feed the hungry. They suggested that Katie give the cabbage to Tri County Family Ministries, a local **soup kitchen**.

The soup kitchen eagerly accepted Katie's gift. That one cabbage, along with some ham and rice, fed 250 hungry people. Katie went to the soup kitchen and helped serve the meal. When she saw how much good one cabbage could do, Katie decided to grow a vegetable garden to help feed people in need. Katie began planning. She wanted to create a big garden and give away the vegetables.

Katie's cabbage weighed 40 pounds (18 kilograms).

In their own words

Eleanor Roosevelt, **first lady** of the United States from 1933 to 1945, was an author, **diplomat**, and **humanitarian**. She once said: "It is not fair to ask others [to do] what you are unwilling to do yourself."

Growing the project

The next summer, Katie grew more vegetables. She gave her harvest to people in need. She wanted to do more, but seeds and equipment are expensive. Family, friends, and classmates helped. So did community organizations, seed companies, and local farmers.

In 2009, Katie began her own **nonprofit organization**, Katie's Krops. She developed a website to explain her project and to encourage others to start their own vegetable gardens for the hungry. Katie also received **grants** to help buy seeds. By 2011, Katie had established six gardens in her community. Katie wants to see gardens like hers providing food to hungry people everywhere.

This is one of six gardens that Katie sponsors in her hometown.

In their own words

Katie says, "My advice is to follow your heart. If you find a cause you truly believe in, you should do your best to help and you will make others happy as well as yourself. Doing something to help others makes your heart happy!"

Katie's entire school helps to plant, harvest, and distribute food from the school garden.

Kids who made a difference

In 1946, when Asfaw Yemiru was nine years old, he began living on the streets of Addis Ababa, Ethiopia's capital city. A kind woman took him in and sent him to school. At age 14, Asfaw began teaching other poor children to read. By the time he was 17, over 200 children attended his classes. Eventually, Asfaw raised money for school buildings and supplies. His free schools have educated thousands of poor children.

Katie is committed to helping the hungry, but she knows she cannot solve this problem alone. Her family and classmates help plant, weed, and harvest vegetables. Lisa Turocy, an experienced gardener, gives Katie gardening advice. Turocy says, "If I can help her change the world, that's awesome."

Spreading the word

Katie's project, like her garden, continues to grow. In 2011, Katie planned to offer two grants to young gardeners, but over 200 applied. Katie received so many great proposals that she increased the number to seven full grants and three smaller grants. Katie has won several awards for her efforts, but she says that the greatest reward comes from helping others.

Top tips

Even if you cannot grow your own garden, you can help feed the hungry. Why not collect canned food for a **food bank** or participate in a fund-raising event? Some food organizations need volunteers to sort food items and pack them for delivery. Soup kitchens often need volunteers to prepare and serve meals. Find what works best in your own community.

To learn more about her project, visit Katie's website at www.katieskrops.com.

Helping to fight hunger

According to the World Hunger Organization, 925 million people around the world suffered from hunger in 2010. That is one out of every seven people. Children are at the greatest risk. Poor nutrition can cause learning disabilities, poor health, blindness, and death. About 5 million children die each year from causes related to hunger.

In May 2010, children in Paris, France, participated in a race to raise money to help feed people in need.

Salim Sheikh: Mapping the Slum

Salim Sheikh and his friends worked for over a year to put their community on the map. Salim lives in the Rishi Aurobindo Colony, a community in Kolkata, India. Kolkata has one of the world's largest **slums**, with a population of about 1.5 million people. Rishi Aurobindo Colony is located within the slum.

Salim lives in Kolkata, a city in eastern India.

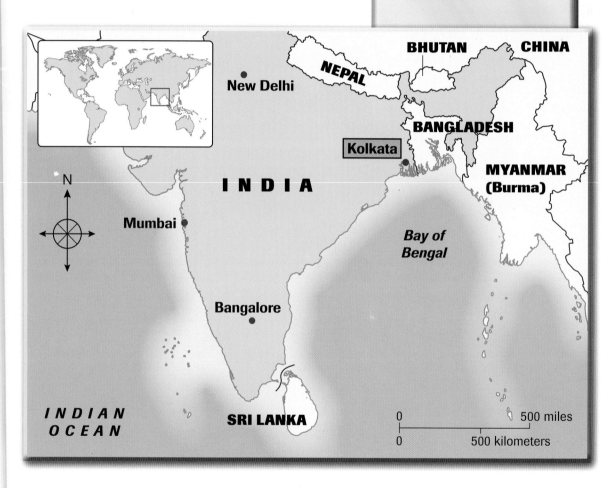

Slums are heavily populated, run-down sections of cities. About one in three city dwellers lives in a slum. Most slums lack basic services such as running water, electricity, and garbage collection. Slum houses are often unsafe and crowded closely together. As more and more of the world's people move to cities, the number of people living in slums will increase.

Giving young people a voice

In the past, slums were not included on city maps. Officials ignored India's slums. Salim's maps show overcrowded conditions and a lack of schools, hospitals, and other important services. The maps help communities to identify the services they need.

Salim is participating in a UNICEF program called Awaaz Do (Speak Up). Awaaz Do gives young people an opportunity to improve their communities and better the lives of many people.

The students in Kolkata's slums worked in groups to gather information.

In their own words

Martin Luther King, Jr., the **civil rights** leader, once said, "Everybody can be great. Because anybody can serve. You don't have to have a college degree to serve . . . . You only need a heart full of grace. A soul generated by love."

Doing research

Salim worked on a team with three other young people. Each team included a photographer, note-takers, and a mapmaker. At each home, they asked:

* How many people live in the home?
* How old are they?
* What work do they do?
* Do they have any particular health problems?

They took notes and photographed water pumps, crowded alleys, trees, temples, schools, and power sources.

People who live in slums, like this one in Kolkata, often lack adequate schools, health care, and clean water.

After they gathered the information, Salim and his group created colorful, hand-drawn maps. The maps will be uploaded to Google Earth so that everyone can learn about Rishi Aurobindo Colony.

In their own words

Salim says, "With this map, everyone in the world will know we are here. We are a community with many issues and ideas, just like anybody."

Getting results

After Salim and his friends completed their maps, community leaders showed the maps to local officials. They used the maps to discuss particular problems in the slum. For example, the maps identified 71 water sources, but not a single one was safe for drinking. The maps provided community leaders with the proof they needed to convince city officials of their problems. Salim hopes that the maps will lead to improvements.

Top tips

Is there a problem in your community that is being ignored? If so, consider taking photos, writing an essay, or talking to an official about it. Children's voices can make a huge difference!

Using photography to help

Maps gave Salim a voice. In several other countries, students use photography to help their communities. UNICEF supplies the cameras and encourages young people to take pictures of particular problems. Some young people, like 17-year-old Shuktara Khatun, who lives in Bangladesh, take photos of young children who are working long hours in dangerous jobs. Fifteen-year-old Amadou Keita has taken photographs of working children in the West African country of Mali.

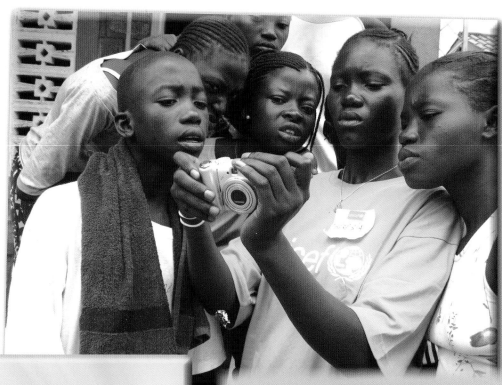

Sixteen-year-old Theresia (holding the camera) photographs her community in the Central African Republic.

In their own words

Chadni Akther, age 14, participated in the photography project in Bangladesh. She said, "Through pictures, I can tell the story of my hardships and the hardships of other children."

Many of the volunteers are children who live and work on the streets. The young people enjoy learning photography. The photos are a powerful tool for change. UNICEF displays the photographs in the cities where the young photographers live and in special exhibitions in major cities, such as Tokyo and New York.

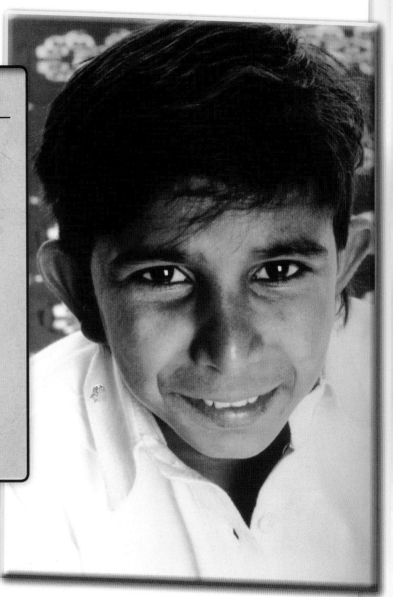

Kids who made a difference

In 1987, four-year-old Iqbal Masih (right) was forced to work in a carpet factory in Pakistan for 12 to 14 hours a day. If he refused to work, he was beaten. He escaped when he was 10 and began speaking about the terrible conditions faced by child **slaves** like himself. Iqbal's speeches brought worldwide attention to this problem and helped free hundreds of child workers. Very sadly, on April 16, 1995, 12-year-old Iqbal was murdered because of his courageous efforts to help the world's working children.

Ashlee Smith: Bringing Comfort

Ashlee Smith knows how it feels to lose everything. When she was six years old, a fire damaged Ashlee's home in Nevada. All her toy horses, stuffed animals, and books had to be thrown out because of severe smoke damage. Ashlee felt sad and depressed. Two years later, Ashlee's experience and the news of another fire spurred her to action.

Ashlee's dad was a firefighter. In 2007, when Ashlee was eight, her dad and other firefighters were fighting the Angora Fire in nearby South Lake Tahoe. He sent pictures on his cell phone that showed burned toys and melted tricycles. "I knew how those kids felt, and I just wanted to make a difference," said Ashlee. She began collecting toys to replace the things that the children had lost in the fire.

Ashlee lives in Sparks, Nevada, as shown on this map.

CANADA

Sparks

NEVADA

New York

Washington D.C.

UNITED STATES

Los Angeles

PACIFIC OCEAN

ATLANTIC OCEAN

N

MEXICO

GULF OF MEXICO

0   500 miles

0   500 kilometers

Here, Ashlee is collecting toys.

Helping kids

Ashlee's mother told her that other things were more important than toys. But Ashlee disagreed. She saw the problem from a child's point of view, and toys are important to children. Several organizations provided food and shelter. They worked with the adults, but Ashlee wanted to focus on the children. "I just feel like kids sometimes get put to the side; kids have feelings and are depressed about what's happened, too," she said. Ashlee began contacting local radio stations and asking people to contribute toys.

In their own words

Former British **prime minister** Winston Churchill once said, "We make a living by what we get, but we make a life by what we give."

Helping one child at a time

Within a few weeks of the Angora Fire, Ashlee had collected thousands of toys. When she began handing them out, Ashlee noticed one small girl reaching for a particular puzzle. It was exactly like one she had lost in the fire. The little girl's smile convinced Ashlee that she was doing something of value for children who had suffered losses. She was making a difference!

Ashlee's dream got bigger. She stood outside stores asking for donations, she spoke on local radio programs, and she created flyers telling people about her project. By 2010, she had given over 175,000 toys to children who had lost their homes to fires, floods, or other natural disasters.

Ashlee's dad's work as a firefighter helped inspire her project, which she called Ashlee's Toy Closet.

Helpful strangers

Ashlee's hard work brought rewards. She was featured in magazine and newspaper articles. She appeared on national television programs. Ashlee used her newfound fame to expand her program. People sent contributions from all over the country. Toy companies donated toys, and moving companies offered to deliver toys to disaster areas. Ashlee has been amazed by the kindness and generosity of strangers who are eager to help. She thanks her family, too, and the neighbors who continue to support her.

Ashlee says stuffed animals and books are favorites among the kids she helps.

In their own words

When asked to give advice to other young people, Ashlee said, "It's not that difficult. You can make a huge difference in someone's life by touching just one person's heart. It makes the world a better place."

Moving ahead

Just as Katie Stagliano set up her own charity, Katie's Krops, Ashlee also established a nonprofit organization. Her website keeps **contributors** informed of her latest projects, needs, and sponsors. In addition to helping children in her own state of Nevada, Ashlee has expanded her program to other areas of the United States and the world. In 2010, Ashlee collected funds to help rebuild three **orphanages** in Haiti that had been destroyed in an earthquake. She also offers toys to parents who cannot afford to buy birthday gifts for their children.

Top tips

Sharing is great, but no one wants broken and dirty items. When you contribute toys, clothes, or other items to people in need, send things that are in good condition. New is best, but gently used is fine, too. Sometimes it is most helpful to send money so that people can buy what they really need.

To learn more about her project, visit Ashlee's website at www.ashleestoycloset.org.

In the spring of 2011, Ashlee began collecting toys for children in Joplin, Missouri, after a tornado destroyed homes there. Ashlee believes that with every toy, she also hands out hope. She wants children to know that they have not been forgotten.

When a tornado struck Joplin, Missouri, Ashlee began collecting toys for children who had lost everything.

In their own words

Bishop Desmond Tutu won the Nobel Peace Prize in 1984 for his efforts to bring peace to his nation of South Africa. He once said, "Do your little bit of good where you are; it's those little bits of good put together that overwhelm the world."

Ryan Hreljac: Providing Clean Water

In 1998, six-year-old Ryan Hreljac's teacher told him that people in faraway places were dying because they did not have clean water. Ryan decided to do something about it. His teacher said that a well would cost about $70. Ryan asked his parents for the money, but they did not give it to him. They made him earn it by doing jobs like washing windows and vacuuming the floors. It took him four months to earn $70.

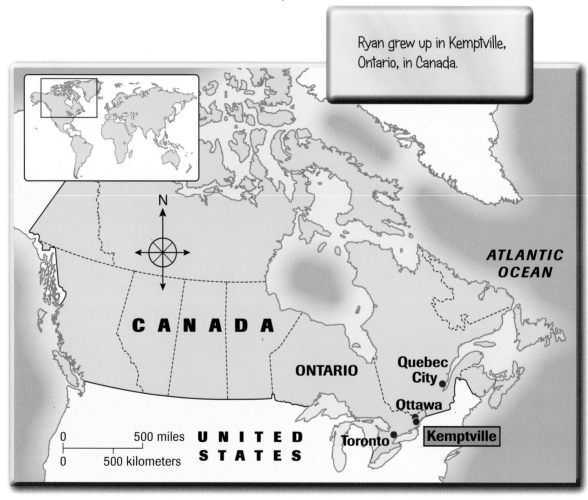

Ryan grew up in Kemptville, Ontario, in Canada.

That's when Ryan learned that $70 would only buy the hand pump that sits on top of the well. A complete well would cost around $2,000. So Ryan did more jobs. A local newspaper ran a story about Ryan's project, and people started sending donations. By January 1999, Ryan had enough money to pay for an entire well near an elementary school in Agweo, Uganda.

The problem

While he was earning the money, Ryan learned more about water problems around the world. Nearly one in eight people do not have access to clean water. Every single day, about 4,500 children die from drinking unsafe water. Many others become sick or live in poor health. Babies and children are in the greatest danger. In many areas of the world, children walk miles to collect water, and the only water they can find is dirty.

In their own words
Albert Schweitzer, a German doctor who founded a medical clinic in West Central Africa, said, "Do something wonderful, people may imitate it."

Ryan was nine years old when he first visited Uganda to see his well.

Speaking out

Ryan learned that digging wells by hand is difficult. For about $25,000, he could buy a power drill that would make digging wells in Uganda quicker and simpler. To raise more money, Ryan began talking to school children about the need for clean water wells in Africa. The more Ryan spoke about his dream of providing clean water to the world, the more other children and adults joined the cause. Soon Ryan's story appeared in national newspapers and on television.

When Ryan was nine, he visited his well in Agweo, Uganda. People greeted him with cheers. His well had made Agweo a healthier place. People now had clean water for drinking, cooking, and washing.

In 2006, Ryan returned to Uganda to see his wells in action.

Ryan's Well

In 2001, Ryan and his supporters created a nonprofit organization called Ryan's Well **Foundation**. Ryan spoke all over the world. He not only raised money, but he also taught people about the importance of clean water.

In addition to building wells, Ryan's foundation also teaches people how to take care of the well and how to keep water clean by building **latrines** (outdoor toilets) far from wells. By 2011, Ryan's Well Foundation had built wells and latrines that benefit 723,375 people in 16 different countries. Projects continue in several African countries and in Haiti.

Clean water can be the difference between life and death for some people.

Person to person

Ryan not only helped to build wells and latrines, but he also connected with the people of Uganda. Ryan's teacher arranged for him and his classmates to write to children in Uganda. When Ryan visited in 2000, he met his pen pal, Jimmy Akana. The two boys became friends. When Ryan learned that Jimmy's life was in danger, Ryan and his family arranged to bring Jimmy to Canada. Jimmy became a brother to Ryan, and the boys continue to work together to help others.

A well that provides clean drinking water is important for keeping a community healthy.

Working together

Although Ryan worked hard, he could not have accomplished his goals alone. One of Ryan's aims is to motivate people to help others. Makenzie Conner, age 17, wanted to help others, too. She worked with the Water Project. Like Ryan's Well, the Water Project is a nonprofit organization that builds wells. In 2011, Makenzie, who lives in Michigan, raised $1,000 for the Water Project as part of a school assignment.

When a third grader named Sam Decker read about Makenzie's success in the local newspaper, he called her and asked if she would help him raise money for clean water. Sam's teacher had given each student one dollar to "change the world." Mackenzie was happy to help. Sam used his dollar to make signs and cans for donations. He raised $104. By working together, Makenzie and Sam made a difference!

To learn more about Ryan's Well Foundation, visit its website at www.ryanswell.ca.

Top tips

If you want to raise money for charity, set yourself a goal. For example, you might aim to raise $20, or maybe you think you could raise $100! Having a goal will keep you motivated to keep going until you reach your target.

You Can Make a Difference

On his 17th birthday, pop star Justin Bieber asked family, friends, and fans to contribute $17 in his honor to a clean water project in **developing nations**. "Even if you don't have $17 to give," he told fans, "I just ask you to go out in your community and try and make a positive difference. Even the smallest act of kindness can go a long way." Over 2,000 fans raised $47,544 for clean water.

You don't need to be famous to help others. Matt Pearce, Dionne Burns, and Jared Vigil were not famous. They used skills they had learned to help others in need. Katie Stagliano and Salim Sheikh learned the new skills of gardening and mapping to help their communities. Ashlee Smith and Ryan Hreljac learned about a particular problem and took steps to solve it. They had to raise money to reach their goals. Raising money is not easy, so it is not the right choice for everyone. What will you do to help? The choice is yours.

Talia Leman was 10 years old when she began helping others.

Kids who made a difference

Talia Leman was 10 years old in August 2005 when Hurricane Katrina destroyed thousands of homes in New Orleans and the surrounding area. Talia decided to help. She encouraged children all over the United States to "trick-or-treat for Katrina." They raised over $10 million. Talia wanted to do more, so she started a project called RandomKid. It helps young people organize fund-raising projects. Children and teenagers using Talia's website (see page 47) have raised money for hundreds of different projects.

These kids are running a marathon in Ramallah, Palestine, to raise money for local children's projects.

Making a Difference Map

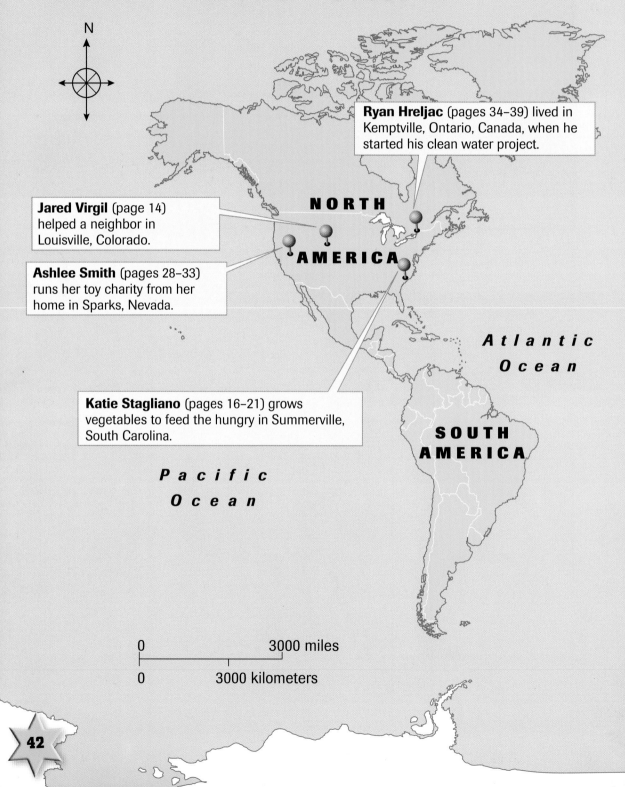

Arctic Ocean

N

Ryan Hreljac (pages 34–39) lived in Kemptville, Ontario, Canada, when he started his clean water project.

NORTH AMERICA

Jared Virgil (page 14) helped a neighbor in Louisville, Colorado.

Ashlee Smith (pages 28–33) runs her toy charity from her home in Sparks, Nevada.

Atlantic Ocean

Katie Stagliano (pages 16–21) grows vegetables to feed the hungry in Summerville, South Carolina.

SOUTH AMERICA

Pacific Ocean

0   3000 miles

0   3000 kilometers

Dionne Burns (page 12) helped save a life in Glasgow, Scotland.

Matt Pearce (pages 10–15) helped a stroke victim in Longlevens, England.

Salim Sheikh (pages 22–27) helped map his neighborhood in Kolkata, India.

Chadni Akther (page 27) takes photos in Bangladesh to help improve children's lives.

Amadou Keita (page 26) takes photos in Mali to help child workers.

Tilly Smith (page 15) was on vacation in Phuket, Thailand, when she warned people about a tsunami.

Asfaw Yemiru (page 19) has set up schools in Addis Ababa, Ethiopia.

Ryan Hreljac's first well was dug in Uganda.

Arctic Ocean

ASIA

EUROPE

AFRICA

Pacific Ocean

Indian Ocean

AUSTRALIA

Southern Ocean

ANTARCTICA

43

Tips on Making a Difference

Are you ready to help? If so, here are a few tips about what to do:

Find the right project for you

One way to help is to join a project that's already up and running. It is important to choose one that matches your interests, skills, and talents. If you truly believe in a project, it will be easier to commit your time and energy to it.

* Talk to friends, parents, and teachers. What organizations do they support? Why? Do any of their causes interest you?

* Watch for announcements in school or in the community about local charity events. Local organizations such as soup kitchens or children's hospitals often hold fund-raising events and ask for volunteers.

Choosing a charity

It is important to research a charity before you donate your money or time. An adult can help you do this. Here are some tips:

* First, find a charity that helps a cause you are interested in. Websites such as www.charitynavigator.com allow you to search charities by topic.

* Find out how the charity uses its money. Does most of it go to the people who need it? There are websites listed on page 47 that can help you find out.

* Once you have chosen a charity, find out what help they need. Some are looking for volunteers, while others need donations of money or goods.

44

Starting your own project

If you cannot find the right project, you might want to start your own. This can be a big job, so don't be afraid to ask for help! Learn as much as you can about the problem you want to solve. Is there anyone else in your community or elsewhere who is working toward the same goals? You might be able to learn from these people or even get their support. Once you decide on a particular project, develop a plan to reach your goal.

Talk with a trusted adult

Many of the young people featured in this book had help and support from their parents and other trusted adults. You should discuss your idea with a parent, teacher, or club leader. Adults will help you stay safe. They can provide advice and check to see that any organization you want to help is worthy of your time and effort.

Involve others

Working together leads to success—there is strength in numbers! When starting a new project, try to find people who share your goals and will help you. You may be surprised at how eager your family, friends, and classmates are to lend a hand.

Glossary

charity organization that raises money for those in need

civil rights rights of people to be equal to others and have political and social freedom

community service project specific task designed to help others

contributor someone who gives money, goods, or help to a project

developing nation country where the average income is much lower than in industrial nations like the United States

dike long wall or embankment built to stop flooding from the sea

diplomat government official who deals with foreign countries

donation gift of money, goods, or help to a person or project

first aid emergency medical care

first lady wife of the U.S. president

food bank charity that gives out donated food to the hungry

foundation organization that provides funds for charity

fund-raise collect money for a specific project

grant sum of money provided for a specific project

humanitarian person who works to improve human welfare

latrine toilet like a trench dug into the ground

moral teaching, lesson, or message

nonprofit organization group that is not intended to make a profit, but is set up to provide a public service

nun woman who belongs to and lives with a religious group

orphanage place that houses and cares for children who do not have parents

paramedic emergency medical worker or doctor

prime minister leader of the government in some countries, such as Canada and the United Kingdom

recycle treat or process materials so that they can be used again

slave person who works for another without pay or rights

slum heavily populated, run-down section of a city

soup kitchen place where food is served at little or no cost to the needy

sponsor give money or help to a charity or good cause. A company or organization that supports a project is also called a sponsor.

symptom sign of a medical problem

tsunami unusually large sea wave produced by an earthquake or undersea volcanic eruption

UNICEF (United Nations Children's Fund) United Nations organization devoted to the needs of children throughout the world

Find Out More

Books

Guillain, Charlotte. *101 Ways to Be a Great Role Model* (101). Chicago: Raintree, 2012.

Gutwein, Austin, and Todd Hillard. *Take Your Best Shot: Do Something Bigger Than Yourself.* Nashville: Thomas Nelson, 2009.

Olien, Rebecca. *Kids Care!: 75 Ways to Make a Difference for People, Animals and the Environment.* Nashville: Williamson, 2007.

Shoveller, Herb. *Ryan and Jimmy and the Well in Africa That Brought Them Together.* Tonawanda, N.Y.: Kids Can, 2008.

Websites

Visit the Water Project at: **thewaterproject.org**

Investigate possible ways to help others through RandomKid at:
www.randomkid.org

Learn more about UNICEF at: **www.unicef.org**

The following websites all help to match people with volunteer activities in their area or elsewhere:
www.dosomething.org
www.idealist.org
www.volunteermatch.org

The following websites are useful places to go if you want to find out more about a particular charity or organization:
www.charitynavigator.org
www.givewell.org
www2.guidestar.org

At this website, you can read reviews of nonprofit organizations and also add your own:
www.greatnonprofits.org

Index